# Is that a Rash?

Dr. Alvin Silverstein,

Virginia Silverstein, and

Laura Silverstein Nunn

## My Health

**Franklin Watts**

*A Division of Grolier Publishing*

New York • London • Hong Kong • Sydney

Danbury, Connecticut

Content Consultant
**Stephen B. Webster, M.D.**
Gunderson Lutheran Medical Center
Medical Professor of Dermatology
University of Minnesota

Cartoons by Rick Stromoski; medical illustration by Leonard Morgan
Photographs©: Envision: 30 left (George Mattei); Medichrome/StockShop: 29
(Anatomyworks/Marcia Hartsock); Monkmeyer Press: 40 (Capece), 16
(Dollarhide), 13 right (Siteman); Peter Arnold Inc.: 15 bottom (Zeva Oelbaum);
Photo Researchers: 35 (Biophoto Associates), 4 (Biophoto Associates/Science
Source), 32 (Scott Camazine), 30 right (Tim Davis), 27 (Dr. Brian Eyden/SPL), 9, 11
left, 13 left (David Gifford/SPL), 28 (John Kaprielian), 6 right, 19, 36, 39 (Dr. P.
Marazzi/SPL), 6 left (Oliver Meckes), 34 (Oliver Meckes/Gelderblom), 38 (Science
Photo Library), 8 (Quest/SPL), 18 (James Stevenson/SPL), 11 right (Vision); Scott
Camazine: 15 top, 15 center, 33 (Sue Trainor); The Image Works: 21 (Bill
Bachmann), 20 (Nancy Richmond); Visuals Unlimited: 37 (Kenneth Greer), 25 (M.
J. Johnson).

Visit Franklin Watts on the Internet at:
http://publishing.grolier.com

**Library of Congress Cataloging-in-Publication Data**

Silverstein, Alvin.
    Is that a rash? / by Alvin Silverstein, Virginia Silverstein, and Laura
Silverstein Nunn.
        p.   cm.—(My health)
    Includes bibliographical references and index.
    Summary: Describes various types of rashes with information on how they
affect people, how they spread, and how to treat them, including some rashes
associated with childhood diseases.
    ISBN 0-531-11637-9 (lib. bdg.)          0-531-16541-9 (pbk.)
    1. Urticaria—Juvenile literature. [1. Skin—Diseases. 2. Skin—Inflammation. 3.
Skin—Infections] I. Silverstein, Virginia  II. Nunn, Laura Silverstein.   III. Title.
IV. Series.
RF249.S57      1999
616.5'1—dc21                                                      98-53648
                                                                                      CIP
                                                                                      AC

GROLIER
PUBLISHING

# Contents

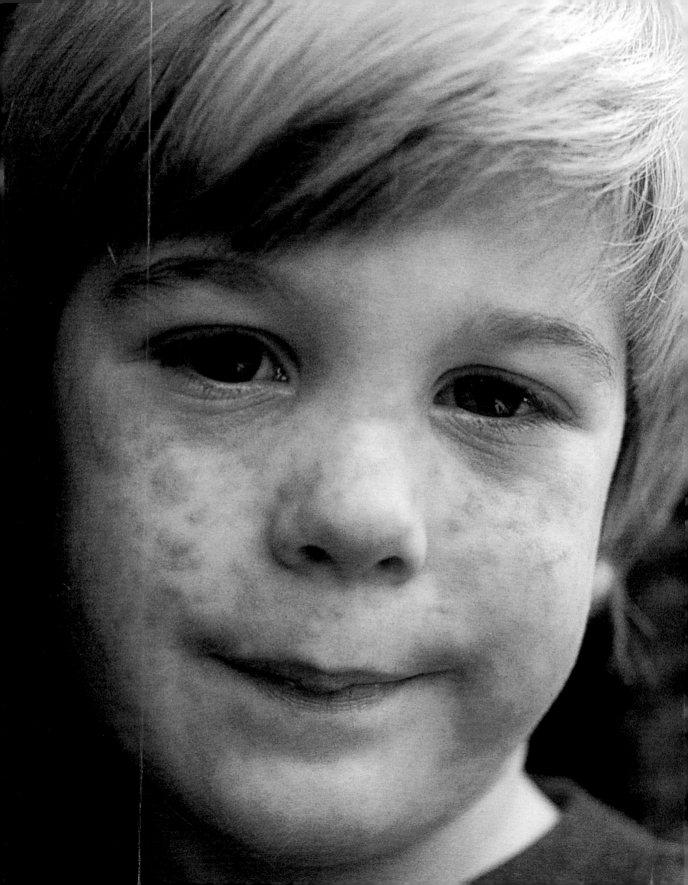

# Signs of Trouble

Do you get red, itchy bumps when you touch poison ivy? Or maybe you get **hives** when you eat chocolate? Have you ever had **chickenpox** or **measles**? Was your body ever covered from head to toe with yucky, itchy **blisters**?

Most of the time, your skin is probably clear and fairly smooth. But sometimes it may get red, bumpy, or spotted. When it does, you have a **rash**! Everybody gets rashes now and then. Rashes are a kind of warning. They let you know that your body is being harmed in some way.

**Did You Know...**

More than 1,000 diseases and conditions can affect your skin. Many of them cause rashes.

◀ **What kind of rash is this?**
**Measles.**

5

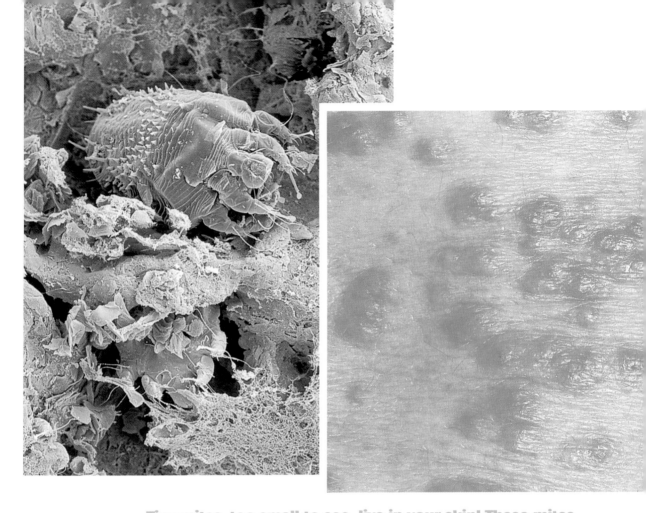

Tiny mites, too small to see, live in your skin! These mites cause a rash called scabies (left). The scabies rash (right), caused by mites that live and burrow in the skin, is very itchy.

Many things can cause rashes. It could be something you touch, eat, or breathe that makes your skin break out in a rash. Some illnesses, such as scarlet fever and Lyme disease, cause rashes. Tiny creatures, such as bacteria and itch **mites**, can cause rashes too. What a rash looks like and where it shows up can help doctors figure out what has caused it.

# The Skin We Live In

You may not think your skin is as important as your heart, lungs, kidneys, or brain. But your skin is actually your largest organ, or body part, and it has many important jobs.

Your skin protects you by keeping dangerous chemicals and most germs from getting inside your body. At the same time, it keeps the fluids you need inside, so that your body will not dry out. Your skin also helps keep your temperature steady. It gives off heat in hot weather and holds in warmth when it is cold outside. Your skin is also a sense organ. It tells you a lot about the world around you.

Your skin is made up of billions of tiny cells that are too small to see without a microscope. You probably think all your skin cells are alive. That would seem to make sense. After all, as you grow, your skin grows with you. But actually, some of the cells in your skin are dead. The average skin cell lives only 28 days, and new cells are constantly forming inside your skin.

As new cells form, they push the dead ones up toward the outside of your body. The dead cells are squeezed together and flattened to form a thick, tough outer layer. These dead cells are mostly made of a **protein** called *keratin.*

Your living skin cells are nourished by millions of tiny *blood vessels.* These blood vessels carry

The cells at the top of the skin are flattened and dead. They form a tough covering that protects the living cells underneath.

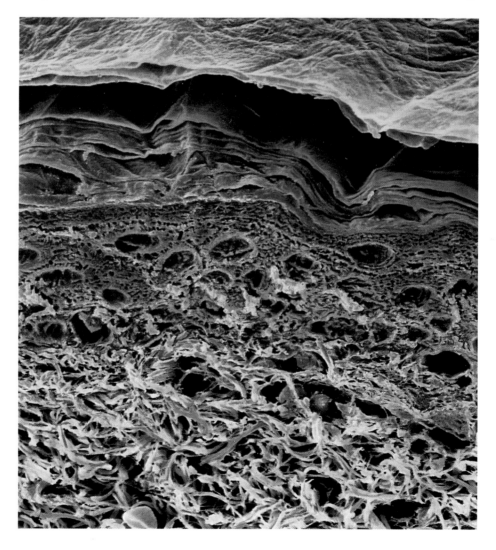

8

food and oxygen to your skin and take away waste products. Your skin also contains **nerve endings,** which send messages to your brain about the world around you. With a single touch, you can tell if an object is rough or smooth, hot or cold. If you

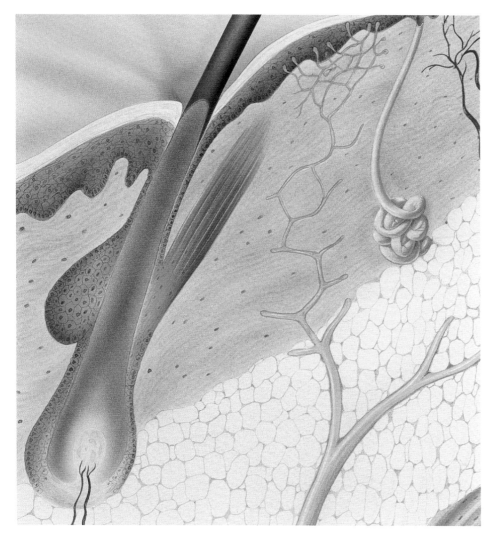

This diagram of the skin shows a hair follicle, a sweat gland, a nerve fiber network (yellow), and blood vessels (red and blue) running through the skin and the fatty layer beneath it.

# Why Do We Blush?

Can you tell when people are nervous, embarrassed, or scared? Their skin may tell you. Anger, excitement, or embarrassment may cause a person to blush. When this happens, the person's face turns a rosy color. The skin looks red because nerve messages make blood vessels in the skin widen and carry more blood. Have you ever blushed? You probably noticed that your skin felt hot. This is because the blood carries heat from the inner parts of your body to your skin.

touch something that is too hot, or sharp enough to hurt you, nerve endings send out pain messages that may make you say "Ouch!" Other nerves carry messages to the skin. Some of them cause blood vessels to widen and carry more blood. Others pull on tiny muscles around the hairs on your skin to give you "goosebumps."

Your skin has two kinds of **glands**—tiny organs that produce fluids that empty out to the surface.

**Sweat glands** are shaped like tiny coiled tubes. They are found all over your body, but especially under your armpits and on the palms of your hands. These glands produce a watery fluid called sweat. The sweat pours out of tiny sweat **pores** (openings) in your skin and helps keep your body cool by carrying away heat.

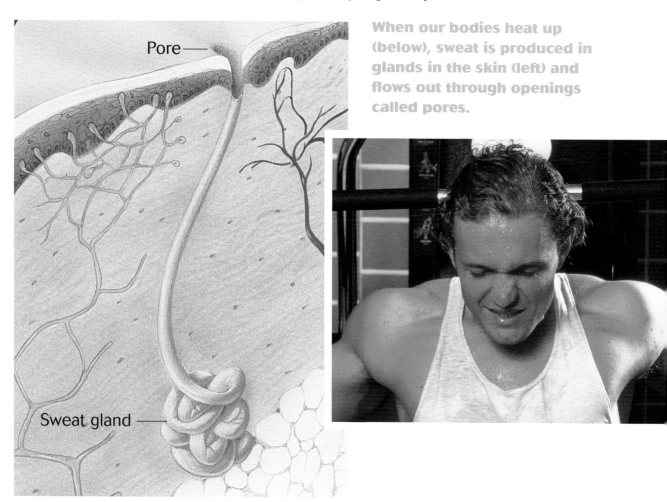

When our bodies heat up (below), sweat is produced in glands in the skin (left) and flows out through openings called pores.

Pore

Sweat gland

Sebaceous glands, or oil glands, produce an oily substance called sebum. Sebum keeps your skin and hair soft and smooth. Most oil glands empty into tubelike hair follicles. Every strand of hair on your body grows out of a separate hair follicle. A bulb at the bottom of each hair follicle holds the "root" of the hair. The bulb is the only part of the follicle that

# The Microworld on Your Skin

Would you believe that you have billions of tiny creatures living in and on your skin? They are so small that you need a microscope to see them. Some of these microscopic creatures are bacteria. They can be found all over your body, feeding on dead cells and waste products. Some bacteria feed on the chemicals in sweat, especially in places like the armpits. Underarm sweat has a bad odor because smelly chemicals are produced when bacteria break down sweat.

Mites, tiny relatives of spiders, also find food and shelter in people's skin. Face mites, or follicle mites, live in the hair follicles on the face, but they rarely come onto the surface of the skin. Even when they do, you won't notice them because they are too small to see without a magnifying glass. These mites are often found in the hair follicles of the eyebrows—so it's a good idea to wash your eyebrows regularly.

contains living hair cells. The hair you see above the surface of your skin is not alive. Like the outer layer of your skin, hair is mostly made of keratin.

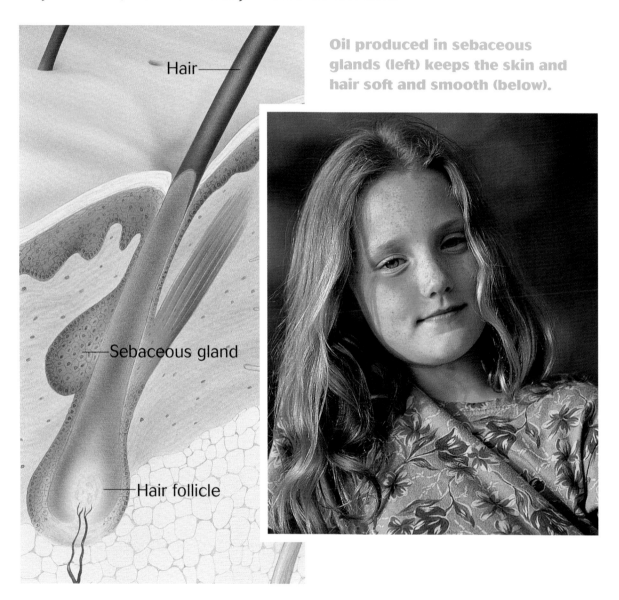

Oil produced in sebaceous glands (left) keeps the skin and hair soft and smooth (below).

Hair

Sebaceous gland

Hair follicle

# What Are Rashes?

Rashes break out when your skin becomes irritated or **inflamed** (swollen). Doctors use the medical terms **dermatitis** or **eczema** to describe rashes. Both these words mean "inflammation of the skin."

Inflammation develops when body cells are hurt. The damaged cells send out chemical alarm signals to call for help. These chemicals cause the walls of the tiny blood vessels in the skin to widen and get leaky. Fluid from the blood seeps out into the tissues, which causes the skin to become inflamed.

Rashes are usually red and itchy, but they can vary greatly. Some may be raised bumps that look like pimples. Others may be flat, red blotches or itchy, oozing blisters. Still others are patches of rough, scaly skin.

## Did You Know...

If the word "inflammation" sounds a lot like "flame," there's a good reason. The inflamed tissues in the skin are not only swollen, they are often hot and red too.

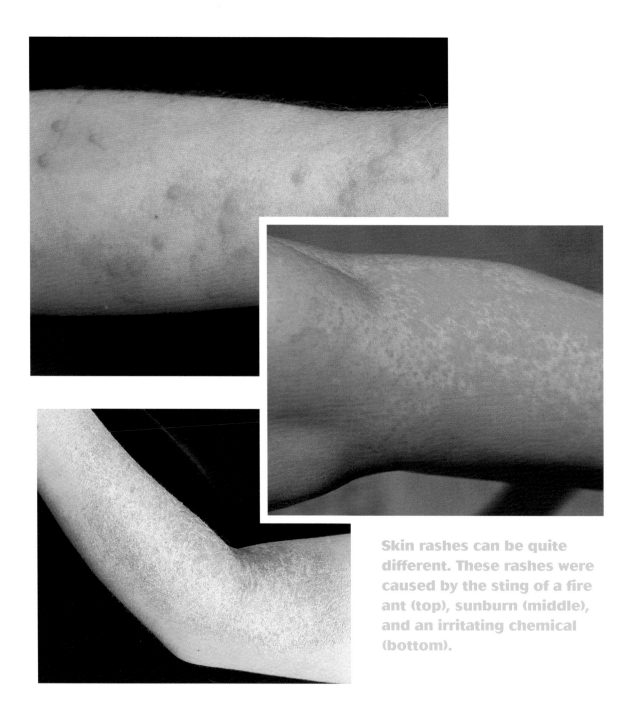

Skin rashes can be quite different. These rashes were caused by the sting of a fire ant (top), sunburn (middle), and an irritating chemical (bottom).

Many things can cause rashes.

- Some people get rashes from chemicals or tiny creatures that come into contact with the skin.
- Allergies can cause rashes. Your body may react to something you have touched, eaten, or breathed in.
- Rashes are sometimes a symptom of an illness or disease. Rashes often help doctors identify an illness, depending on where the rash is and what it looks like.
- Some people break out in a rash when they are emotionally stressed—nervous, upset, or excited.

If this girl were allergic to wool, the scarf and hat might produce a rash on her face.

# Activity 1: Who Has Rashes?

You can find out more about rashes by taking a survey of your friends and relatives. Try to include people of different ages and both sexes. Ask each person the following questions:

Have you ever had a rash? If so, what did it look like? How long did it last?

Did you take any medicine or other treatment for it?

Do you have allergies? If so, what are you allergic to?

Did you ever have measles, rubella (German measles), or chickenpox?

Have you ever been immunized against any of these diseases by getting a shot, for example?

Medical experts estimate that at least 20 percent of people have allergies. How do your results compare? (They may be quite different, because the number of people you questioned was much smaller than the number of people studied by scientists.) You may find that nearly everyone in the older age groups had measles, rubella, and chickenpox, but almost none of the children have had measles and rubella. That is because most children today get **vaccines** to prevent these common diseases. There was no vaccine against chickenpox until 1995, so there are still many children who have had the disease.

# Close Contact

Every person's skin is different. Some people have sensitive skin that is easily irritated. Other people's skin that is less likely to be harmed by **irritants.** What kind of skin do you have?

We are surrounded by all kinds of chemicals. Many of them can cause rashes when they come into contact with the skin. As the number of chemical-containing products increases, more and more people are finding substances that affect their skin.

This rash was caused by an allergy to a leather wrist strap.

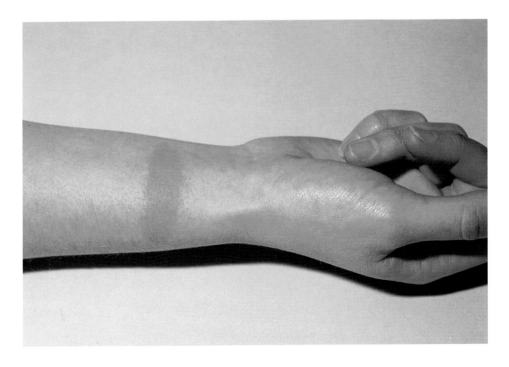

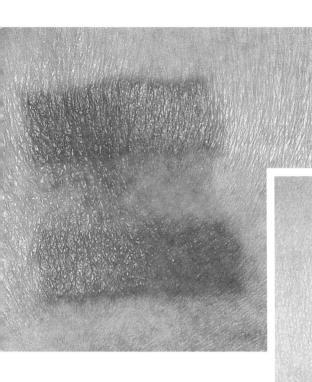

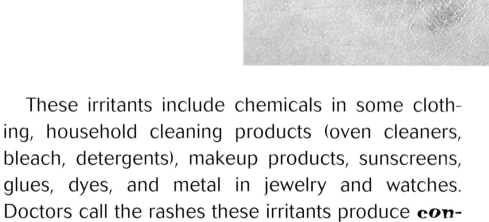

Allergies to the adhesive in a bandage (left) or the metal in a wristwatch (below) can also produce rashes.

These irritants include chemicals in some clothing, household cleaning products (oven cleaners, bleach, detergents), makeup products, sunscreens, glues, dyes, and metal in jewelry and watches. Doctors call the rashes these irritants produce **contact dermatitis.**

What can you do to protect your skin from irritants? The first step is to find out what is irritating your skin.

The chemicals in new clothes can produce a rash on sensitive skin, so it is best to wash clothes before wearing them.

Then try to avoid it. Many brand-new clothes contain chemicals, for example. So if you have sensitive skin, wash new clothes before you wear them for the first time. If you use cleaning products, wear gloves to protect your hands. There are many ways you can protect yourself, although it is not always easy.

Do you ever get a rash when you are hot and sweaty? Many infants and children do. **Prickly heat,** also called heat rash, is a skin condition that occurs when the skin is hot and moist. When your skin gets hot, you start to sweat. That's normal. But if your skin is covered, the sweat cannot escape and your sweat pores become clogged. The next thing you know, you have a rash.

Heat rash looks like tiny red bumps. It can occur anywhere on the body, but it is most common in the creases of the skin, which are not exposed to the air.

Like heat rash, **diaper rash** occurs because moisture is trapped next to the skin. But in diaper rash, the chemicals in the baby's urine and stools also help to irritate the skin.

Prickly heat and diaper rash are not serious conditions, but if they are left untreated, oozing blisters can develop. Both types of rashes can be prevented and treated by keeping the skin cool and dry. For heat rash, wear loose clothing and keep cool. You can put calamine lotion on a rash to dry it out. For diaper rash, babies should be changed frequently to keep them dry.

As you read earlier, many kinds of microscopic creatures live in or on your skin. Normally, they live happily on dead skin or waste products on your body, doing no harm. But sometimes these tiny critters can cause trouble for you and your skin.

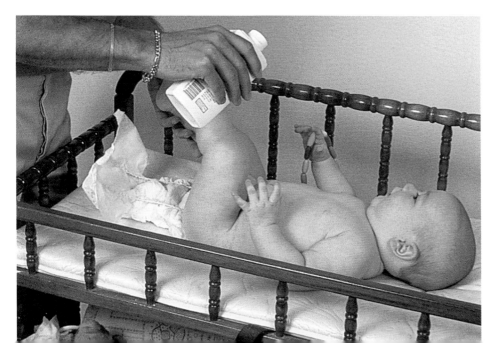

Changing diapers frequently can help prevent diaper rash.

# Troublemakers in the Skin

| Condition | Description |
|---|---|
| Impetigo  | Very **contagious**; common in children. Tiny oozing blisters may appear anywhere on the body, but are found mostly on the hands and the face. They usually form on skin that has already been damaged by an allergic rash or cut. If the blisters are scratched, the rash can spread from one area of the body to another. Impetigo can also be spread to other family members by sharing clothing, towels, and bedsheets. |
| Scabies  | Very contagious; can be passed to another person through direct contact or by sharing towels or bedsheets. Mites' eggs and waste products cause a reaction in the skin. A zigzag blister trail marks where a female mite laid her eggs. The rash is itchy, especially at night. |
| Ringworm  | Very contagious; can be passed to another person through direct contact with an infected person or dog. The name "ringworm" describes the thin, ringlike rash that forms on the skin. The rash is red, scaly, and itchy. Ringworm of the skin usually appears on the arms, feet, and shoulders. Other kinds of ringworm can affect other parts of the body, including the scalp, feet, and nails. |

| Creatures Responsible | Treatment |
| --- | --- |
| Bacteria 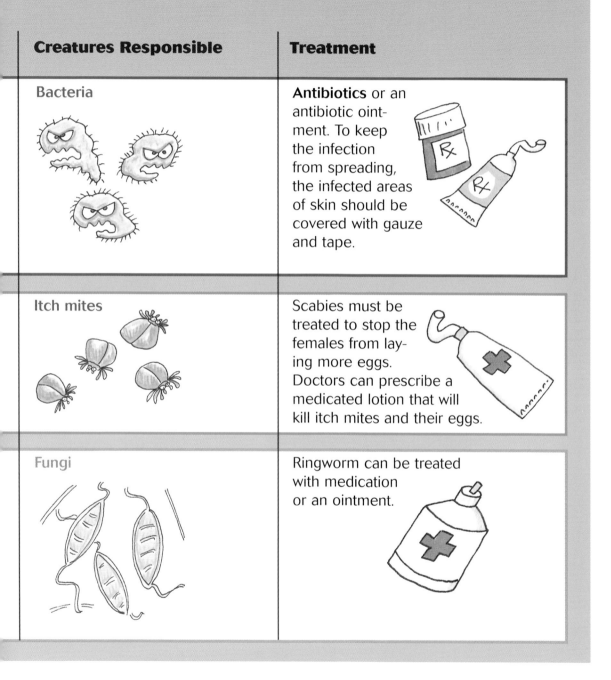 | **Antibiotics** or an antibiotic ointment. To keep the infection from spreading, the infected areas of skin should be covered with gauze and tape. |
| Itch mites | Scabies must be treated to stop the females from laying more eggs. Doctors can prescribe a medicated lotion that will kill itch mites and their eggs. |
| Fungi | Ringworm can be treated with medication or an ointment. |

# Allergy Rashes

While some substances are irritating enough to cause a rash in anybody's skin, allergy rashes affect only people with extra-sensitive skin. These people are **sensitized** to certain substances. The slightest exposure causes an allergic reaction in a sensitized person.

An allergy is your body's overreaction to a substance that is normally harmless. The substance that causes the allergic reaction is called an **allergen**. An allergen may get into your body when you touch it, breathe it in, or eat it, or when it is injected into your skin.

Allergic reactions happen when your body's defenses, the **immune system,** overreact to foreign substances in the body. Normally, the immune system's job is to protect the body from any foreign invaders, such as disease germs that make you sick. An army of soldiers, the

## Did You Know...

It may take several exposures for you to become sensitized to a substance. In fact, it may take days, weeks, or even years to develop an allergy.

24

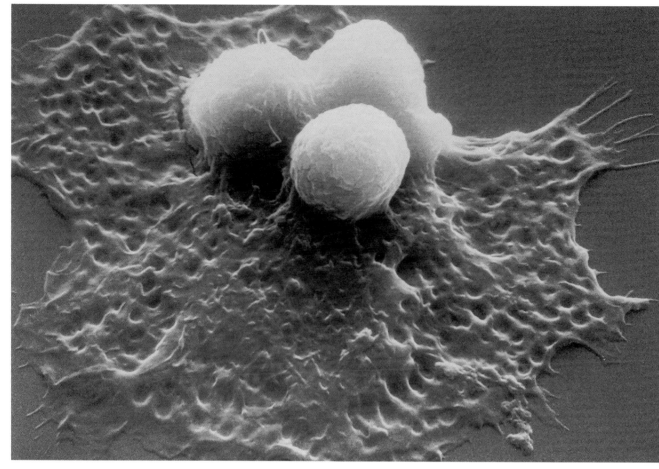

In this magnified picture, a white blood cell is attacking three cancer cells.

**white blood cells**, fight these invaders. They travel in the bloodstream and can even slip through the gaps between body cells. The white blood cells can detect foreign substances that have chemicals different from those of normal body cells.

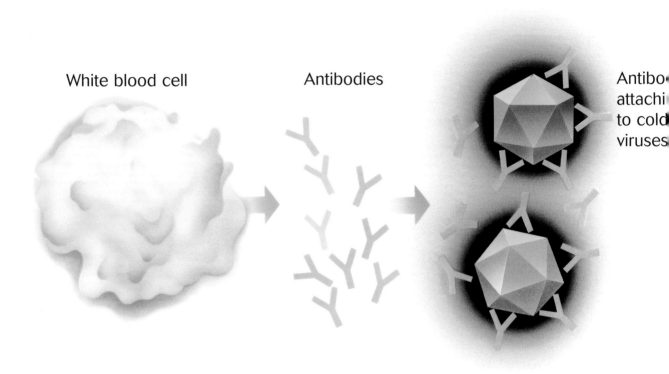

White blood cell       Antibodies       Antiboattachi
to cold
viruses

When germs invade your body, some white blood cells produce antibodies. The antibodies attach to the germs and
help destroy them.

Once a foreign chemical has been identified, some
immune cells make proteins called **antibodies.**
Antibodies are like ammunition for the white cell soldiers. They may damage invading germs or make it easier for the white blood cells to catch and kill the germs.

After the battle is over, some of the antibodies stay
in the body. Then, if the same kind of germs invade
again, the antibodies against them can be used as a

pattern to quickly make a new supply of antibodies. People who have antibodies against a particular invader do not catch the illness that it causes.

People who have allergies make antibodies that contain a material called **IgE.** These IgE antibodies are found in the nose, the throat, the lungs, the stomach, and the skin. They can attach to cells called **mast cells,** which are found in the same places as the IgE antibodies. When IgE antibodies that are attached to mast cells latch onto certain allergens—watch out! The mast cells send out a chemical called **histamine.** Histamine causes some of the body's tissues to become inflamed—red and swollen. If this happens in the skin, you break out in a rash.

When IgE antibodies attached to this mast cell (green) come into contact with an allergen, the cell will release histamine (red).

Many things can cause allergic reactions. Did you ever get a terrible itchy rash a few days after touching poison ivy? If you did, you're not alone. Poison ivy plants are the most common cause of allergic reactions in the United States. About 90 percent of all people are allergic to the sticky oil of the poison ivy plant and its relatives—poison oak and poison sumac. You can get a poison ivy rash even if you don't touch the plant itself. You can get a poison ivy rash from petting

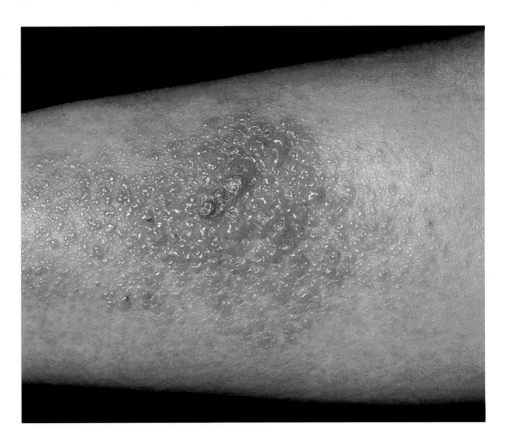

This rash was caused by touching poison ivy.

# The Poison Plants

- Poison ivy grows in low shrubs, vines, or climbing vines. It has groups of three shiny leaves, greenish flowers, and white berries.
- Poison oak is a low bushy plant with groups of three oak-like leaves, yellow-green flowers, and white berries.
- Poison sumac is a tall, skinny shrub or tree with 7 to 13 smooth-edged leaves and white berries.

**The poison plants: sumac (upper left), ivy (upper right), and oak (bottom).**

a dog, touching a friend, or picking up a baseball that came into contact with the plant.

What else can cause an allergic rash? The list goes on and on. Like contact dermatitis, allergic reactions can be caused by things you have contact with every day. These include certain types of fabrics (wool, silk, or fur), fabric softeners, dyes, rubber, leather, metal, glues, paints, soaps, detergents, and some kinds of lotions.

Allergy rashes may also be caused by things you eat. Common foods that can cause rashes include nuts, fish and shellfish, milk, eggs, pork, strawberries, oranges, and bananas. Drugs such as aspirin and penicillin may also cause rashes.

Rashes may even be caused by things we breathe in, such as pollen, house dust, molds, and animal dander—tiny flakes of skin. Sensitized people do not need close contact to get a rash—just breathing the allergens in the air can cause a rash.

Eating one of these foods can make some people break out in a rash (above). Some people are allergic to the dander from pets (right).

# Activity 2: Are You Sensitive?

**Warning:** *If you know you are allergic to any of the materials listed below, do not use them in the test. If you have a cut or a scratch on your arm, do not put test patches over it. If you notice any redness or pain around any of the spots before the test time is over, remove that test patch immediately and wash your skin thoroughly with soap and water.*

Dab a small amount of peanut butter on the inside of your forearm. Put a bit of skin lotion or cream on another spot. Tape a small piece of wool cloth or yarn on another spot, a piece of raw apple or other fruit on another, a flower petal or a plant leaf (*not* poison ivy!) on another, and a nickel on another spot.

Wait 20 minutes, then take each test substance off and look at your skin. Are there any red or swollen spots? If so, write down what substance caused them, and tell your doctor about them at your next visit.

You probably will not notice any reaction to any of the substances in this test, but some people are allergic to each of these things—or even to the tape used to place them on the skin.

This girl's eye was swollen shut by an allergic reaction after a bee stung her on the cheek.

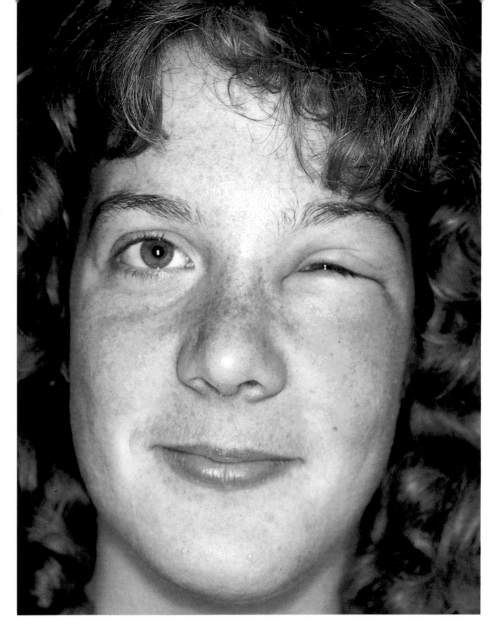

Things that are injected into our bodies, such as the **venom**, or poison, in insect stings, may cause allergic rashes. Most people have a normal reaction to bee stings—a little swelling around the red, itchy area of the sting. But people who are allergic to bee stings

# What Are Hives?

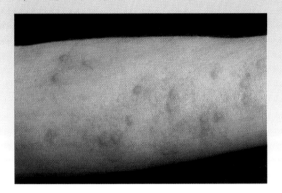

Hives are caused by an allergic reaction. They are usually caused by something you ate, a medicine you took, something you breathed in, an insect sting, or an infection in the body.

**The red swellings on this person's arm are hives.**

may develop a much more serious rash. Sometimes allergic reactions to bee stings are very dangerous and quick medical treatment is necessary.

What can you do about allergies? If possible, avoid the allergen. If you can't, try to reduce your exposure to it. For instance, if you are allergic to ragweed pollen, stay indoors with the windows closed. If it is impossible to stay away from an allergen, you can treat your allergies with a wide variety of drugs, including antihistamines. Antihistamines stop the harmful effects of histamine in the body. Allergy shots can also reduce a person's sensitivity to certain allergens.

33

# Itchy Illnesses

Some illnesses are famous for their rashes. Many of these itchy illnesses are caused by **viruses.** These disease germs are so tiny that you need a microscope to see them. Many of them enter your body through your nose or mouth. As you learned earlier, your immune system works hard to get rid of invaders, and that includes viruses. In the meantime, however, you feel just awful.

The chicken-pox viruses shown at the top of this picture are magnified more than 20,000 times.

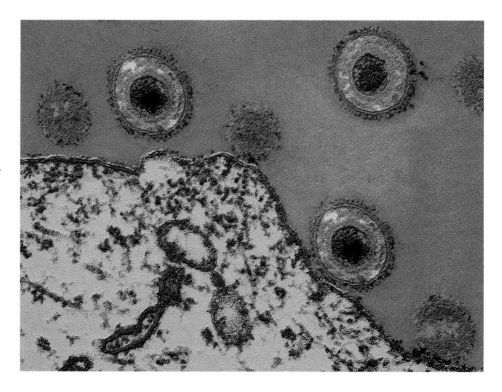

Chickenpox is a very common childhood illness with an easily recognized rash. It is caused by a virus. For the first few days, you have cold-like symptoms, a cough, and a fever. Then a rash with red spots appears. Chickenpox spots can cover the entire body and cause terrible itching. The spots later turn into cloudy blisters, break open, and then crust over. It is very important not to scratch the blisters because they can become infected and cause scars.

Chickenpox is very easy to catch. In the past, most children got chickenpox before the age of 10. Now that there is a chickenpox vaccine, more children can be protected against this irritating disease.

The chickenpox rash looks different from the red rashes of some other common illnesses. These other diseases are often lumped together in a list of common childhood illnesses because they all seem to have similar red rashes.

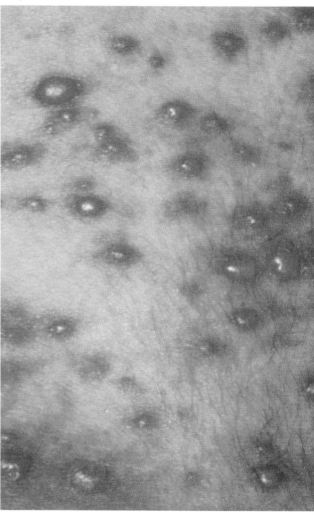

Chickenpox produces a blistery, itchy rash.

Measles is the best known of these diseases. Measles is caused by a virus. About 10 days after exposure, a person feels tired and sick with a fever, a runny nose, a cough, and red eyes. Several days later, flat reddish-brown spots appear on the face and then spread to the rest of the body. Eventually, the spots join together to form large blotches.

Measles is very contagious. It can be much more serious in teenagers and adults than in children. So it is very important to get measles shots as early as possible.

Rubella is a contagious disease that produces a red rash similar to the measles rash. Some people call rubella "German measles," but the virus that causes rubella is not related to the measles virus. Rubella is also called "3-day measles" because, unlike regular measles, it goes away fairly quickly. Rubella is a much milder disease than measles. The symptoms may be so mild that a person may not even feel sick. Some people who have rubella do not even develop a rash.

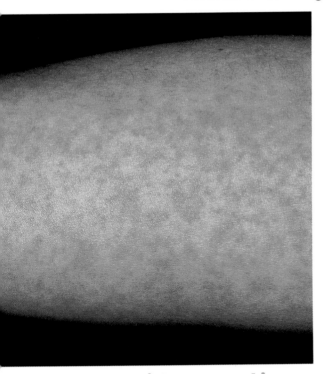

The small pink spots on this woman's arm are a rash caused by rubella.

The first signs of rubella appear 2 to 3 weeks after exposure to the virus. Symptoms may include a runny nose, red eyes, a slight fever, a headache, and swollen lymph nodes. The rubella rash is usually made up of small pink dots that stay separated and it lasts only about 1 to 3 days. Children should be vaccinated against rubella as early as possible so that they will not get this disease.

# Bull's-eye!

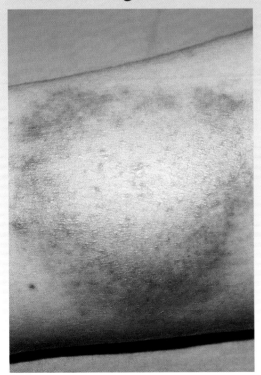

Rash illnesses are sometimes confused because the rashes they produce look very similar. But sometimes the rash is so different that doctors can quickly identify the problem. **Lyme disease,** a bacterial illness transmitted by ticks, has a very unusual rash. It looks like a bull's-eye, with rings of red and pale skin around the tick bite. However, some people with Lyme disease do not get this bull's-eye rash.

**A rash with rings of red and pale skin may appear after a tick carrying Lyme disease bites a person.**

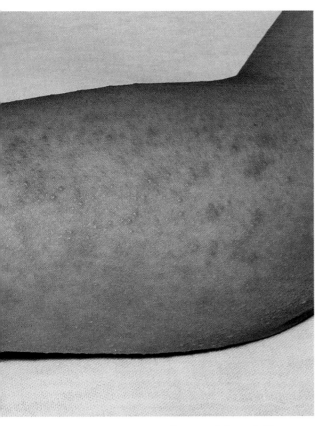

The scarlet rash on this girl's arm shows how scarlet fever got its name.

**Scarlet fever** is another contagious disease that produces a red rash. It can be very dangerous. Until the 1940s, scarlet fever was almost as common as measles and many people died of it. Unlike many other rash diseases, scarlet fever is caused by a bacterium, not a virus. The same bacterium causes strep throat.

The early symptoms of scarlet fever include a very bad sore throat, a high fever, and a headache. Next, a pinkish red rash appears on the face, the neck, the chest, and spreads to the rest of the body. The tongue also turns strawberry colored—a white coating with red spots. After a few days, the symptoms usually go away, and the skin peels. Fortunately, scarlet fever can easily be treated with antibiotics.

**Roseola infantum** is another red rash disease. It occurs mainly in children between 6 months and 2 years old. It almost never affects anyone over 4 years old. Roseola is a fairly mild disease and is caused by a virus. It starts with a high fever that lasts 2 to 3 days. After the fever goes down, a rosy red rash appears on the face, the neck, the arms, and the rest of the body. The rash usually doesn't last more than 2 days. It may disappear in just a few hours.

**Fifth disease,** as its name suggests, is fifth on the list of common childhood rash illnesses. Fifth disease is sometimes called slapped-cheek disease because for the first day or two its bright red rash makes the person's face look like it has just been slapped. Then a lacy red rash appears on the arms, the legs, and the trunk. Fifth disease has mild symptoms, so no treatment is needed.

Can you see why fifth disease is sometimes called slapped-cheek disease?

To keep your skin healthy, wash it regularly, eat the right foods, and get plenty of rest.

By now you must realize that your skin is pretty amazing. If you keep your skin clean, provide it with important vitamins and minerals, and get plenty of rest, your skin will take care of you. It will protect you from dangerous chemicals and germs, keep the fluids you need inside your body, maintain your body temperature, and help you sense the world around you.

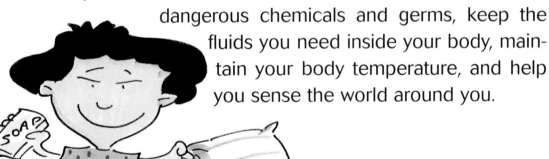

# Glossary

**allergen**—a substance that causes an allergic reaction

**antibiotic**—a medication that kills bacteria

**antibody**—a protein produced by white blood cells; some antibodies help to kill germs

**bacterium** (plural **bacteria**)—a microscopic single-celled organism; some bacteria can cause illness

**blister**—a lump on the skin that contains a watery liquid

**blood vessel**—a tube that carries blood through the body

**chickenpox**—a viral disease with a rash in the form of pimplelike spots

**contact dermatitis**—a skin rash caused by contact with an irritant

**contagious**—can be spread by direct contact with someone already infected with it

**dermatitis**—inflammation of the skin; a rash

**diaper rash**—a rash that a baby may develop due to the moist conditions and contact with irritants in the urine or diaper

**eczema**—inflammation of the skin; a rash

**fifth disease**—a mild viral disease that produces a bright red rash on the cheeks, followed by a lacy red rash on the arms, the legs, and the trunk; also called slapped-cheek disease

**gland**—an organ or group of cells specialized for producing and releasing a substance that does some job in the body or passes out of the body

**hair follicle**—the tubelike structure in the skin from which a hair grows

**histamine**—a chemical released by mast cells that causes tissues to become inflamed

**hive**—a red, itchy swelling caused by an allergic reaction

**IgE**—the material within some antibodies that play a role in allergic reactions

**immune system**—the body's disease-fighting system

**inflamed**—red, swollen, and warm. Skin becomes inflamed when it is injured or infected.

**irritant**—a substance that produces inflammation

**keratin**—a protein found in skin, hair, and nails

**Lyme disease**—a bacterial disease carried by ticks. It often produces a "bull's-eye" rash of red and pale rings around the site of the tick bite.

mast cell—a kind of cell in the skin and lining tissues (such as in the breathing passages) that binds IgE antibodies and releases histamine and other inflammation chemicals

measles—a viral disease with a red, blotchy rash

mite—a small, eight-legged animal related to spiders

nerve ending—the tip of a nerve cell. When a nerve ending senses a change in the skin, it sends a message to the brain.

pore—the opening of a skin gland

prickly heat—a rash that forms most often in creases and folds of the skin under hot, sweaty conditions

protien—a substance found in all plant and animal cells. Some proteins help support cells, while others speed up chemical reactions.

rash—an inflammation of the skin. It is usually red and itchy, but it may be scaly, pimpled, or blistered.

roseola infantum—a mild viral disease in very young children, with a rosy red rash

rubella—a viral disease with a rash consisting of small pink dots. It is also called German measles.

scarlet fever—a bacterial disease with a pinkish red rash and "strawberry tongue"

**sebaceous gland**—a skin gland that produces an oily substance, called sebum, that keeps skin and hair soft and smooth. It is also called an oil gland.

**sebum**—the oily substance produced by sebaceous glands, or oil glands, in the skin

**sensitized**—overreacting to a substance after repeated contact with it

**sweat gland**—one of the coiled tubes in the skin that produce a watery substance called sweat. Sweat passes out of the body through openings called sweat pores.

**vaccine**—a substance that stimulates the body's disease-fighting cells to produce antibodies against a particular kind of germ

**venom**—poison produced by an animal such as a spider, a bee, a wasp, or a snake

**virus**—a very tiny living thing that feeds on a living host and reproduces by making the host produce new viruses

**white blood cell**—a jellylike blood cell that can move through tissues and is an important part of the body's defenses. Some white blood cells eat germs and clean up bits of damaged cells and dirt.

# Learning More

**Books**

Ardley, Bridget and Neil. *Skin, Hair, and Teeth.* Englewood Cliffs, NJ: Silver Burdett, 1988.

Knutson, Roger M. *Furtive Fauna.* Berkeley, CA: Ten Speed Press, 1996.

Nourse, Alan E., M.D. *Lumps, Bumps, and Rashes.* New York: Franklin Watts, 1990.

Sandeman, Anna. *Skin, Teeth & Hair,* Brookfield, CT: Copper Beech Books, 1996.

Silverstein, Alvin and Virginia and Robert Silverstein *Overcoming Acne.* New York: Morrow, 1990.

**Organizations and Online Sites**

**American Academy of Allergy, Asthma and Immunology**
611 East Wells Street
Milwaukee, WI 53202
*http://www.aaaai.org/*

**American Academy of Dermatology**
930 Meacham Road
P.O. Box 4014
Schaumburg, IL 60168-4014
*http://tray.dermatology.uiowa.edu/*

**Better Health Healthwise Handbook: Childhood Rashes**
*http://www.betterhealth.com/healthwise/Chapter12/*
*HW_Chapter12d.html*
This site has descriptions of and information about many types of childhood rashes, including chicken pox, diaper rash, fifth disease, prickly heat, roseola, rubella, measles, and scarlet fever.

**MCare: Skin Rashes—Children's**
*http://www.mcare.org/healthtips/homecare/sinkrasa.htm*
Find out about hives, impetigo, poison ivy, and more.

**National Foundation for Infectious Diseases**
Suite 750, 4733 Bethesda Avenue
Bethesda, MD 20814-5228
*http://www.medscape.com/Affiliates/NFID*

**The Yuckiest Site on the Internet: Your Gross and Cool Body—Skin**
*http://www.nj.com/yucky/body/systems/skin/*
This site has all kinds of fun information about human skin. There is even a link to a site with more information about "zits."

# Index

# About the Authors

Dr. Alvin Silverstein is a professor of biology at the College of Staten Island of the City University of New York. Virginia Silverstein is a translator of Russian scientific literature. The Silversteins first worked together on a research project at the University of Pennsylvania. Since then, they have produced six children and more than 150 published books for young people.

Laura Silverstein Nunn, a graduate of Kean College, has been helping with her parents' books since her high school days. She is the coauthor of more than twenty books on diseases and health, science concepts, endangered species, and pets. Laura lives with her husband Matt and their young son Cory in a rural New Jersey town not far from her childhood home.